Selena

A Little Golden Book® Biography

By Maria Correa
Illustrated by Paula Zamudio

🌷 A GOLDEN BOOK • NEW YORK

Text copyright © 2025 by Maria Correa
Cover art and interior illustrations copyright © 2025 by Paula Zamudio
All rights reserved. Published in the United States by Golden Books, an imprint of
Random House Children's Books, a division of Penguin Random House LLC, 1745 Broadway,
New York, NY 10019. Golden Books, A Golden Book, A Little Golden Book, the G colophon,
and the distinctive gold spine are registered trademarks of Penguin Random House LLC.
rhcbooks.com
Educators and librarians, for a variety of teaching tools, visit us at RHTeachersLibrarians.com
Library of Congress Control Number: 2024940863
ISBN 978-0-593-80837-5 (trade) — ISBN 978-0-593-80838-2 (ebook)
Printed in the United States of America
10 9 8 7 6 5 4 3 2 1

Selena Quintanilla (kin-tah-NEE-ya) was born on April 16, 1971, in Lake Jackson, Texas. Her parents, Marcella and Abraham Jr., were Mexican American, which means that Selena's ancestors came from Mexico. Selena had an older brother they called A.B., and an older sister named Suzette.

Music was very important to the Quintanilla family. Selena's father had been in a band called Los Dinos when he was young. He wanted to share his passion for music with his children, so he taught them to play instruments and filled the house with the sounds of his favorite songs.

When Abraham discovered that Selena had a beautiful singing voice, he had an idea: the three kids would form a family band! Selena was the lead singer, A.B. was on bass, and Suzette played the drums. They called themselves Selena y los Dinos, in honor of their father's band.

When Selena was nine years old, her father opened a restaurant called Papagayos, the Spanish word for "parrots." Abraham built a stage there so that the kids could perform while people enjoyed their meals.

Selena y los Dinos were good, but Abraham knew they could be great. He decided that they should focus on playing Tejano music, which Latin American people in Texas loved. There was only one problem: Tejano music was in Spanish, and Selena only spoke English! Her father would have to teach her the language, as well as traditional Tejano songs.

Tejano music was created by Mexican Americans living in Texas in the 1800s. It combines folk music from Mexico, country and Western influences from America, and brass sounds from Europe. Tejano music is typically played by a group of four musicians called a conjunto (kohn-HOON-toh), on accordion, drums, bass, and a twelve-string guitar known as a bajo sexto (BAH-hoh SEX-toh).

Although it was more common for men to play and sing Tejano music, female musicians like Lydia Mendoza, and later, Laura Canales, paved the way for Selena and other women who would make Tejano more popular than ever.

Less than a year after opening the restaurant, the Quintanillas had to close Papagayos. They moved to Corpus Christi, Texas, and now relied on the band to support the family.

Selena y los Dinos played at weddings and fairs, and their popularity grew. The band welcomed new keyboard and guitar players and released its first album, *Mis primeras grabaciones* (*My First Recordings*). They also appeared on a popular Spanish-language TV show called *The Johnny Canales Show*.

In 1986, Selena was named Female Vocalist of the Year at the Tejano Music Awards. She was only fifteen years old!

Selena y los Dinos were becoming famous. It was time to go on tour! The family bought a bus, called it Big Bertha, and traveled across the southwest, playing for large audiences. Although she had to stop going to school after eighth grade, Selena continued her studies by mail and eventually earned her high school diploma.

At around this time, Selena met a talented guitarist named Chris Pérez. The band invited him to join them, and Selena and Chris grew closer. Their friendship blossomed into love, and a few years later, just before Selena turned twenty-one, they married.

Selena's voice captured the attention of a major record company. They made a deal with the band, but they put the spotlight on Selena. Her solo career had begun.

Her first album, *Selena,* came out in 1989, followed by *Ven conmigo* (*Come with Me*) in 1990 and *Entre a mi mundo* (*Enter My World*) in 1992. One of the songs on this album, "Como la flor" ("Like the Flower"), was written by A.B. and would become Selena's most well-known song.

The record company wanted to make Selena
an international superstar. They organized a
concert tour throughout Latin America, starting
in Mexico. Selena was nervous—she had Mexican
roots, but she still didn't speak Spanish perfectly.
Would audiences there accept her and her music?
¡Sí! The tour was a huge success, and Selena
gained thousands of new fans.

In 1994, Selena's album *Live* won the Grammy for Best Mexican American Album. It was the first Tejano album to ever win a Grammy. Soon afterward, Selena released *Amor prohibido* (*Forbidden Love*). One of its hit songs, "Bidi Bidi Bom Bom," was created after Selena made up lyrics on the spot while testing her sound equipment before a performance.

Even though Selena's life revolved around music, she made time for a hobby that also brought her joy: fashion. Selena loved to design her own outfits, and fans loved seeing the memorable looks she wore on stage.

With the help of fashion designer Martin Gomez, Selena turned her ideas into a clothing line and opened two stores in Texas called Selena Etc. Now her fans could listen to her music and dress like her, too! Everything seemed to be going right for Selena.

But on March 31, 1995, things took a tragic turn.
Selena was shot by a woman who had been the
president of Selena's fan club and the manager of
one of her clothing stores. She died shortly after,
only sixteen days before her twenty-fourth birthday.

Thousands of fans gathered outside Selena Etc. to mourn Selena's death. Major TV networks interrupted their programming to share the news. No one could believe she was really gone.

Selena's final album, *Dreaming of You,* was released a few months later. Eager to hear Selena sing again, fans rushed to buy it. The album, which included songs in Spanish and English, sold 175,000 copies the day it went on sale. It topped the charts and introduced Tejano music to millions of people.

Selena continues to be celebrated as a pop culture icon. *Billboard* magazine named her the greatest Latina artist of all time. In 1997, Jennifer Lopez starred in a movie about Selena's life. And in 2017, Selena was honored with her own star on the Hollywood Walk of Fame. At the ceremony, Chris placed a dozen white roses on the star. They were Selena's favorite flower.

Selena's life was brief, but she made the most of her time by doing what she loved: making music. Thanks to her songs and her fans, the Queen of Tejano lives on.

¡Viva, Selena!